THIS
First
Look

Wedding Day Journal Belongs To

Mr & Mrs

_____

Date
_____

DEDICATION

This First Look Wedding Day Notebook is dedicated to all the Lovers out there who love to plan out their wedding day activities, and document their findings in the process.

You are my inspiration for producing books and I'm honored to be a part of keeping all of your wedding day information and records organized.

How to use this First Look Memory Log Book:

This useful first look wedding day memory book is a must-have for anyone that needs to record their wedding day memories! You will love this easy to use journal to track and record all your wedding day activities.

Each interior page includes space to record & track the following:

1. Date - Write down the date of the first look.
2. Private Location - Use this space to fill in the location of the meetup event.
3. Names of Bride and Groom - Record the names of the bride and groom.
4. Weather Conditions - Fill in the space from Sunny to Snowy conditions of the day.
5. Bride's Dress - Stay on task by filling in your dress description.
6. Groom's Wedding Day Attire - Record any notes about the groom's attire.
7. Love Notes - Write down any special love notes from that day.

If you are new to getting married or new to the first look, this memory log book is a must have! Can make a great useful gift for anyone that loves meeting their significant other for a private first look adventure!

Bless!

# First Look

Our Special Prayer Time...

Today I'm grateful for...

Our reflection of this day...

Location of our wedding photos...

Special thank you to my dad...

Special thank you to my mom...

Our secret vows to each other include...

This is just between us, right now I feel...

First Look

Groom's reaction to that first look was...

Bride's reaction to that first look was...

"Our private meeting went like this...

If a blind folded first look, the groom said this...

Some details of the bride's dress to be remembered...

Our first look together, our meeting place was...

The weather on this special day is...

Our wedding theme today is...

Today, My Love, i really want to tell you...

 # First Look

In a year from now, I see us...

3 Reasons I am marrying you today...

"I will always remember from this day forward to...

Notes

 # First Look

Our Special Prayer Time...

Today I'm grateful for...

Our reflection of this day...

Location of our wedding photos...

Special thank you to my dad...

Special thank you to my mom...

Our secret vows to each other include...

This is just between us, right now I feel...

First Look

Groom's reaction to that first look was...

Bride's reaction to that first look was...

"Our private meeting went like this...

If a blind folded first look, the groom said this...

Some details of the bride's dress to be remembered...

Our first look together, our meeting place was...

The weather on this special day is...

Our wedding theme today is...

Today, My Love, i really want to tell you...

First Look

In a year from now, I see us...

3 Reasons I am marrying you today...

"I will always remember from this day forward to...

Notes

First Look

Our Special Prayer Time...

Today I'm grateful for...

Our reflection of this day...

Location of our wedding photos...

Special thank you to my dad...

Special thank you to my mom...

Our secret vows to each other include...

This is just between us, right now I feel...

First Look

Groom's reaction to that first look was...

Bride's reaction to that first look was...

"Our private meeting went like this...

If a blind folded first look, the groom said this...

Some details of the bride's dress to be remembered...

Our first look together, our meeting place was...

The weather on this special day is...

Our wedding theme today is...

Today, My Love, i really want to tell you...

 # First Look

In a year from now, I see us...

3 Reasons I am marrying you today...

"I will always remember from this day forward to...

Notes

First Look

Our Special Prayer Time...

Today I'm grateful for...

Our reflection of this day...

Location of our wedding photos...

Special thank you to my dad...

Special thank you to my mom...

Our secret vows to each other include...

This is just between us, right now I feel...

First Look

Groom's reaction to that first look was...

Bride's reaction to that first look was...

"Our private meeting went like this...

If a blind folded first look, the groom said this...

Some details of the bride's dress to be remembered...

Our first look together, our meeting place was...

The weather on this special day is...

Our wedding theme today is...

Today, My Love, i really want to tell you...

First Look

In a year from now, I see us...

3 Reasons I am marrying you today...

"I will always remember from this day forward to...

Notes

 # First Look

Our Special Prayer Time…

Today I'm grateful for…

Our reflection of this day…

Location of our wedding photos…

Special thank you to my dad…

Special thank you to my mom…

Our secret vows to each other include…

This is just between us, right now I feel…

First Look

Groom's reaction to that first look was...

Bride's reaction to that first look was...

"Our private meeting went like this...

If a blind folded first look, the groom said this...

Some details of the bride's dress to be remembered...

Our first look together, our meeting place was...

The weather on this special day is...

Our wedding theme today is...

Today, My Love, i really want to tell you...

First Look

In a year from now, I see us...

3 Reasons I am marrying you today...

"I will always remember from this day forward to...

Notes

 # First Look

Our Special Prayer Time...

Today I'm grateful for...

Our reflection of this day...

Location of our wedding photos...

Special thank you to my dad...

Special thank you to my mom...

Our secret vows to each other include...

This is just between us, right now I feel...

First Look

Groom's reaction to that first look was...

Bride's reaction to that first look was...

"Our private meeting went like this...

If a blind folded first look, the groom said this...

Some details of the bride's dress to be remembered...

Our first look together, our meeting place was...

The weather on this special day is...

Our wedding theme today is...

Today, My Love, i really want to tell you...

First Look

In a year from now, I see us...

3 Reasons I am marrying you today...

"I will always remember from this day forward to...

Notes

 # First Look

Our Special Prayer Time...

Today I'm grateful for...

Our reflection of this day...

Location of our wedding photos...

Special thank you to my dad...

Special thank you to my mom...

Our secret vows to each other include...

This is just between us, right now I feel...

First Look

Groom's reaction to that first look was...

Bride's reaction to that first look was...

"Our private meeting went like this...

If a blind folded first look, the groom said this...

Some details of the bride's dress to be remembered...

Our first look together, our meeting place was...

The weather on this special day is...

Our wedding theme today is...

Today, My Love, i really want to tell you...

 # First Look

In a year from now, I see us...

3 Reasons I am marrying you today...

"I will always remember from this day forward to...

Notes

 # First Look

Our Special Prayer Time...

Today I'm grateful for...

Our reflection of this day...

Location of our wedding photos...

Special thank you to my dad...

Special thank you to my mom...

Our secret vows to each other include...

This is just between us, right now I feel...

First Look

Groom's reaction to that first look was...

Bride's reaction to that first look was...

"Our private meeting went like this...

If a blind folded first look, the groom said this...

Some details of the bride's dress to be remembered...

Our first look together, our meeting place was...

The weather on this special day is...

Our wedding theme today is...

Today, My Love, i really want to tell you...

First Look

In a year from now, I see us...

3 Reasons I am marrying you today...

"I will always remember from this day forward to...

Notes

 # First Look

Our Special Prayer Time...

Today I'm grateful for...

Our reflection of this day...

Location of our wedding photos...

Special thank you to my dad...

Special thank you to my mom...

Our secret vows to each other include...

This is just between us, right now I feel...

First Look

Groom's reaction to that first look was...

Bride's reaction to that first look was...

"Our private meeting went like this...

If a blind folded first look, the groom said this...

Some details of the bride's dress to be remembered...

Our first look together, our meeting place was...

The weather on this special day is...

Our wedding theme today is...

Today, My Love, i really want to tell you...

 # First Look

In a year from now, I see us...

3 Reasons I am marrying you today...

"I will always remember from this day forward to...

Notes

 # First Look

Our Special Prayer Time...

Today I'm grateful for...

Our reflection of this day...

Location of our wedding photos...

Special thank you to my dad...

Special thank you to my mom...

Our secret vows to each other include...

This is just between us, right now I feel...

First Look

Groom's reaction to that first look was...

Bride's reaction to that first look was...

"Our private meeting went like this...

If a blind folded first look, the groom said this...

Some details of the bride's dress to be remembered...

Our first look together, our meeting place was...

The weather on this special day is...

Our wedding theme today is...

Today, My Love, i really want to tell you...

 # First Look

In a year from now, I see us...

3 Reasons I am marrying you today...

"I will always remember from this day forward to...

Notes

 # First Look

Our Special Prayer Time...

Today I'm grateful for...

Our reflection of this day...

Location of our wedding photos...

Special thank you to my dad...

Special thank you to my mom...

Our secret vows to each other include...

This is just between us, right now I feel...

First Look

Groom's reaction to that first look was...

Bride's reaction to that first look was...

"Our private meeting went like this...

If a blind folded first look, the groom said this...

Some details of the bride's dress to be remembered...

Our first look together, our meeting place was...

The weather on this special day is...

Our wedding theme today is...

Today, My Love, i really want to tell you...

 # First Look

In a year from now, I see us...

3 Reasons I am marrying you today...

"I will always remember from this day forward to...

Notes

 # First Look

Our Special Prayer Time...

Today I'm grateful for...

Our reflection of this day...

Location of our wedding photos...

Special thank you to my dad...

Special thank you to my mom...

Our secret vows to each other include...

This is just between us, right now I feel...

First Look

Groom's reaction to that first look was...

Bride's reaction to that first look was...

"Our private meeting went like this...

If a blind folded first look, the groom said this...

Some details of the bride's dress to be remembered...

Our first look together, our meeting place was...

The weather on this special day is...

Our wedding theme today is...

Today, My Love, i really want to tell you...

First Look

In a year from now, I see us...

3 Reasons I am marrying you today...

"I will always remember from this day forward to...

Notes

 # First Look

Our Special Prayer Time...

Today I'm grateful for...

Our reflection of this day...

Location of our wedding photos...

Special thank you to my dad...

Special thank you to my mom...

Our secret vows to each other include...

This is just between us, right now I feel...

First Look

Groom's reaction to that first look was...

Bride's reaction to that first look was...

"Our private meeting went like this...

If a blind folded first look, the groom said this...

Some details of the bride's dress to be remembered...

Our first look together, our meeting place was...

The weather on this special day is...

Our wedding theme today is...

Today, My Love, i really want to tell you...

 # First Look

In a year from now, I see us...

3 Reasons I am marrying you today...

"I will always remember from this day forward to...

Notes

 # First Look

Our Special Prayer Time...

Today I'm grateful for...

Our reflection of this day...

Location of our wedding photos...

Special thank you to my dad...

Special thank you to my mom...

Our secret vows to each other include...

This is just between us, right now I feel...

First Look

Groom's reaction to that first look was...

Bride's reaction to that first look was...

"Our private meeting went like this...

If a blind folded first look, the groom said this...

Some details of the bride's dress to be remembered...

Our first look together, our meeting place was...

The weather on this special day is...

Our wedding theme today is...

Today, My Love, i really want to tell you...

First Look

In a year from now, I see us...

3 Reasons I am marrying you today...

"I will always remember from this day forward to...

Notes

First Look

Our Special Prayer Time...

Today I'm grateful for...

Our reflection of this day...

Location of our wedding photos...

Special thank you to my dad...

Special thank you to my mom...

Our secret vows to each other include...

This is just between us, right now I feel...

First Look

Groom's reaction to that first look was...

Bride's reaction to that first look was...

"Our private meeting went like this...

If a blind folded first look, the groom said this...

Some details of the bride's dress to be remembered...

Our first look together, our meeting place was...

The weather on this special day is...

Our wedding theme today is...

Today, My Love, i really want to tell you...

# First Look

In a year from now, I see us...

3 Reasons I am marrying you today...

"I will always remember from this day forward to...

Notes

First Look

Our Special Prayer Time...

Today I'm grateful for...

Our reflection of this day...

Location of our wedding photos...

Special thank you to my dad...

Special thank you to my mom...

Our secret vows to each other include...

This is just between us, right now I feel...

 # First Look

Groom's reaction to that first look was...

Bride's reaction to that first look was...

"Our private meeting went like this...

If a blind folded first look, the groom said this...

Some details of the bride's dress to be remembered...

Our first look together, our meeting place was...

The weather on this special day is...

Our wedding theme today is...

Today, My Love, i really want to tell you...

 # First Look

In a year from now, I see us...

3 Reasons I am marrying you today...

"I will always remember from this day forward to...

Notes

 # First Look

Our Special Prayer Time...

Today I'm grateful for...

Our reflection of this day...

Location of our wedding photos...

Special thank you to my dad...

Special thank you to my mom...

Our secret vows to each other include...

This is just between us, right now I feel...

First Look

Groom's reaction to that first look was...

Bride's reaction to that first look was...

"Our private meeting went like this...

If a blind folded first look, the groom said this...

Some details of the bride's dress to be remembered...

Our first look together, our meeting place was...

The weather on this special day is...

Our wedding theme today is...

Today, My Love, i really want to tell you...

 # First Look

In a year from now, I see us...

3 Reasons I am marrying you today...

"I will always remember from this day forward to...

Notes

First Look

Our Special Prayer Time...

Today I'm grateful for...

Our reflection of this day...

Location of our wedding photos...

Special thank you to my dad...

Special thank you to my mom...

Our secret vows to each other include...

This is just between us, right now I feel...

First Look

Groom's reaction to that first look was...

Bride's reaction to that first look was...

"Our private meeting went like this...

If a blind folded first look, the groom said this...

Some details of the bride's dress to be remembered...

Our first look together, our meeting place was...

The weather on this special day is...

Our wedding theme today is...

Today, My Love, i really want to tell you...

 # First Look

In a year from now, I see us...

3 Reasons I am marrying you today...

"I will always remember from this day forward to...

Notes

 # First Look

Our Special Prayer Time...

Today I'm grateful for...

Our reflection of this day...

Location of our wedding photos...

Special thank you to my dad...

Special thank you to my mom...

Our secret vows to each other include...

This is just between us, right now I feel...

First Look

Groom's reaction to that first look was...

Bride's reaction to that first look was...

"Our private meeting went like this...

If a blind folded first look, the groom said this...

Some details of the bride's dress to be remembered...

Our first look together, our meeting place was...

The weather on this special day is...

Our wedding theme today is...

Today, My Love, i really want to tell you...

First Look

In a year from now, I see us...

3 Reasons I am marrying you today...

"I will always remember from this day forward to...

Notes

 # First Look

Our Special Prayer Time...

Today I'm grateful for...

Our reflection of this day...

Location of our wedding photos...

Special thank you to my dad...

Special thank you to my mom...

Our secret vows to each other include...

This is just between us, right now I feel...

First Look

Groom's reaction to that first look was...

Bride's reaction to that first look was...

"Our private meeting went like this...

If a blind folded first look, the groom said this...

Some details of the bride's dress to be remembered...

Our first look together, our meeting place was...

The weather on this special day is...

Our wedding theme today is...

Today, My Love, i really want to tell you...

 # First Look

In a year from now, I see us...

3 Reasons I am marrying you today...

"I will always remember from this day forward to...

Notes

First Look

Our Special Prayer Time...

Today I'm grateful for...

Our reflection of this day...

Location of our wedding photos...

Special thank you to my dad...

Special thank you to my mom...

Our secret vows to each other include...

This is just between us, right now I feel...

First Look

Groom's reaction to that first look was...

Bride's reaction to that first look was...

"Our private meeting went like this...

If a blind folded first look, the groom said this...

Some details of the bride's dress to be remembered...

Our first look together, our meeting place was...

The weather on this special day is...

Our wedding theme today is...

Today, My Love, i really want to tell you...

# First Look

In a year from now, I see us...

3 Reasons I am marrying you today...

"I will always remember from this day forward to...

Notes

 # First Look

Our Special Prayer Time...

Today I'm grateful for...

Our reflection of this day...

Location of our wedding photos...

Special thank you to my dad...

Special thank you to my mom...

Our secret vows to each other include...

This is just between us, right now I feel...

First Look

Groom's reaction to that first look was...

Bride's reaction to that first look was...

"Our private meeting went like this...

If a blind folded first look, the groom said this...

Some details of the bride's dress to be remembered...

Our first look together, our meeting place was...

The weather on this special day is...

Our wedding theme today is...

Today, My Love, i really want to tell you...

First Look

In a year from now, I see us...

3 Reasons I am marrying you today...

"I will always remember from this day forward to...

Notes

# First Look

Our Special Prayer Time...

Today I'm grateful for...

Our reflection of this day...

Location of our wedding photos...

Special thank you to my dad...

Special thank you to my mom...

Our secret vows to each other include...

This is just between us, right now I feel...

 # First Look

Groom's reaction to that first look was...

Bride's reaction to that first look was...

"Our private meeting went like this...

If a blind folded first look, the groom said this...

Some details of the bride's dress to be remembered...

Our first look together, our meeting place was...

The weather on this special day is...

Our wedding theme today is...

Today, My Love, i really want to tell you...

 # First Look

In a year from now, I see us...

3 Reasons I am marrying you today...

"I will always remember from this day forward to...

Notes

First Look

Our Special Prayer Time...

Today I'm grateful for...

Our reflection of this day...

Location of our wedding photos...

Special thank you to my dad...

Special thank you to my mom...

Our secret vows to each other include...

This is just between us, right now I feel...

First Look

Groom's reaction to that first look was...

Bride's reaction to that first look was...

"Our private meeting went like this...

If a blind folded first look, the groom said this...

Some details of the bride's dress to be remembered...

Our first look together, our meeting place was...

The weather on this special day is...

Our wedding theme today is...

Today, My Love, i really want to tell you...

 # First Look

In a year from now, I see us...

3 Reasons I am marrying you today...

"I will always remember from this day forward to...

Notes

 # First Look

Our Special Prayer Time...

Today I'm grateful for...

Our reflection of this day...

Location of our wedding photos...

Special thank you to my dad...

Special thank you to my mom...

Our secret vows to each other include...

This is just between us, right now I feel...

First Look

Groom's reaction to that first look was...

Bride's reaction to that first look was...

"Our private meeting went like this...

If a blind folded first look, the groom said this...

Some details of the bride's dress to be remembered...

Our first look together, our meeting place was...

The weather on this special day is...

Our wedding theme today is...

Today, My Love, i really want to tell you...

First Look

In a year from now, I see us...

3 Reasons I am marrying you today...

"I will always remember from this day forward to...

Notes

# First Look

Our Special Prayer Time...

Today I'm grateful for...

Our reflection of this day...

Location of our wedding photos...

Special thank you to my dad...

Special thank you to my mom...

Our secret vows to each other include...

This is just between us, right now I feel...

 # First Look

Groom's reaction to that first look was...

Bride's reaction to that first look was...

"Our private meeting went like this...

If a blind folded first look, the groom said this...

Some details of the bride's dress to be remembered...

Our first look together, our meeting place was...

The weather on this special day is...

Our wedding theme today is...

Today, My Love, i really want to tell you...

First Look

In a year from now, I see us...

3 Reasons I am marrying you today...

"I will always remember from this day forward to...

Notes

www.ingramcontent.com/pod-product-compliance
Lightning Source LLC
Chambersburg PA
CBHW081156070526
44583CB00021B/2859